WHEN CATS TALK BACK

Cat Cartoons
with Attitude

by Roz Warren

Hysteria Publications
A division of Sourcebooks, Inc.®
Naperville, IL • Bridgport, CT

Published by Sourcebooks, Inc.

P.O. Box 372	P.O. Box 38581
Naperville, IL 60566	Bridgeport, CT 06605
630-961-3900	203-333-9399
Fax: 630-961-2168	Fax: 203-367-7188

ISBN 1-887166-61-0

Printed and bound in the United States of America.

10 9 8 7 6 5 4 3 2 1

This book is dedicated to Rob Haley and Julie Summerfield, the best friends a person or a cat could ever have.

Roberta Gregory

Dean Brittingham

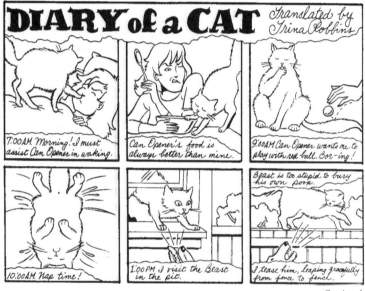

Continued

Anne Beidler

THE PURRIE HOME COMPANION

Roberta Gregory

KITTY KAT TOONS 🐾 🐾

Hey, Muffy. What's wrong?

She YELLED at me again, Smudge! I keep forgetting I'm not supposed to sharpen my claws on the stereo speaker!

You'll have to REALLY show her you're sorry! Give her a GIFT! Catch a nice mouse-bite the head off... and leave it some place she'll know it's just for HER... like on her BEDPILLOW..!

Oh... OKAY!

I always say, try to treat humans as though they're INTELLIGENT...

Hm... there's usually mice in the garage...

Well... is everything okay, now?

NO! THIS time I got yelled at AND SMACKED and she threw me out and threw this mouse right AT me!

WHAT? That's a PERFECTLY good mouse, too! I'd be MAD if I were you! Better complain NOW while she still knows she's done something WRONG!

I know... I'll... PEE under the kitchen table!

Sometimes these humans can be DARN near impossible to figure out...

I'll show HER!

© 1991 Roberta Gregory

Roberta Gregory

Terry Harned

All right, Whiskers, come out
with your claws retracted.

Rina Piccolo

Joan Hilty

"MY CAT SPRAYED EVERYTHING IN THE HOUSE."

Kris Kovick

MORALLY A CAT AND A RAT ARE EQUALS, BUT WHICH ONE WOULD YOU RATHER HAVE IN BED WITH YOU?

Penny Yrigoyen

FOR A MOMENT THEY WERE FROZEN IN TIME
CALLING THE CAT A LAPSED VEGETARIAN WAS A CALCULATED
RISK, AND NEITHER KNEW IF IT WOULD BRING REVENGE
OR REMORSE

Alice Muhlback

Look Dukie, I brought you a friend

Dianne Reum

Chris Suddick

Stephanie Piro

When he told her his cat
was possessed by ELVIS...
She laughed! But later, when
she noticed the sneer...
She wasn't so sure...

After moving to the city, she wondered if she should trade in her cat for a pit bull.

Marian Henley

Cath Jackson

"LOOK. A SUSHI BAR."

Dianne Reum

Nina Paley

CONT. →

CONT. →

CONT. →

Chris Suddick

Rina Piccolo

Cath Jackson

Theresa McCracken

PET PEEVE #37: CAT OWNERS WHO CONSTANTLY DESCRIBE THEIR FELINES' "UNIQUE" ANTICS OVER THE PHONE....

YOU HAD TO **GNAW OFF YOUR OWN FOOT** FOR FOOD, BUT YOU MADE IT TO THE **TOP OF MOUNT EVEREST?** THAT'S GREAT, HONEY, I'M SO PR— OH WAIT— FLUFFY'S **SO CUTE**— SHE'S CHASING HER TAIL AND **PURRING SO LOUDLY!** CAN YOU HEAR HER? WAIT— I'LL PUT HER CLOSE TO THE PHONE. CAN YOU HEAR HER? NO? HOW 'BOUT NOW? NO?

ONLY PHONE IN ALL OF TIBET. HAD TO STAND IN LINE FOR HOURS TO USE IT.

©1991

Judy Becker

Continued

Judy Becker

Continued

Judy Becker

KITTY KAT TOONS 🐾🐾

PFUI! That obnoxious TOMCAT'S back in the neighborhood...

YEEOW! YEEOW

To think that when I was young and foolish, I used to find creeps like him FASCINATING... INTRIGUING...!

REALLY? So did I!

Funny, isn't it?

...and then I started to see guys like him as the jerks they REALLY are...

...seemed to be right after this particularly long trip to the vet!

No fooling? Hey... did you wake up with your belly SHAVED?

YES! And I had these STITCHES that drove me NUTS and I got YELLED at if I tried to lick them..

IT WAS AWFUL!

SAME HERE! ... MY person made me wear a cut-off SOCK around my stomach for a WEEK!

Somehow, this all must tie in to SOMETHING!

Beats ME!

Kathryn Lemieux

Chris Suddick

Lee Kennedy

CAT ACTION COMIX with WOTAN

© L. KENNEDY 91

Marian Henley

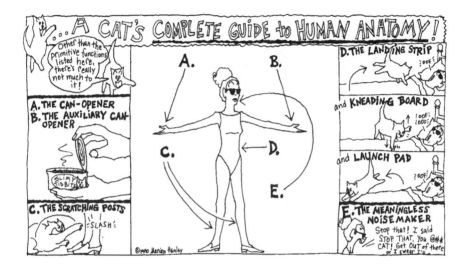

"THERE ARE TWO KINDS OF CAT FUR:
DARK FUR THAT SHEDS ON LIGHT FABRIC,
AND LIGHT FUR THAT SHEDS ON DARK FABRIC."

Marian Henley

Rina Piccolo

Rhonda Dicksion

REMOTE KITTY CONTROL

Roberta Gregory

Andrea Natalie

STONEWALL RIOTS

BY ANDREA NATALIE

Dianne Reum

Dianne Reum

Jennifer Berman

'FESSOR FELINE'S *Cat School*

LESSON #3: COMPANY!

① DOORBELL RINGS. HIDE FOR A LONG TIME.

② COME OUT.

③ DISCOVER THE CAT HATER. BOTHER INCESSANTLY.

TAP TAP

④ FIND FOCAL POINT OF ROOM.

⑤ LICK ANUS.

MORE IMPORTANT GUESTS

IMPORTANT GUEST

⑥ MAKE DISTRACTING SCRATCHING NOISES IN OTHER ROOM.

SCRATCH

RRRIP

SHRED

⑦ GET YELLED AT.

PRICELESS HEIRLOOM

⑧ MAKE CRASHING SOUND

CRASH

⑨ HIDE.

©1988 Jennifer Berman

Jennifer Berman

Viv Quillin

Marian Henley

Lee Binswanger

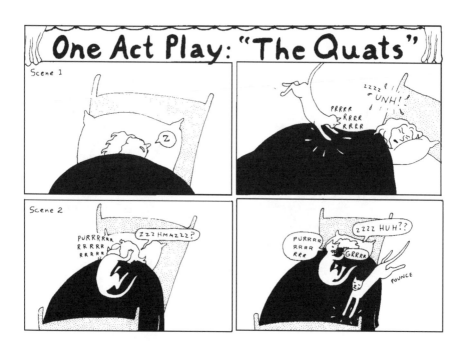

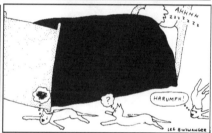

Rina Piccolo

She decided to give up genetic engineering.

Rhonda Dicksion

Fluffy was the only witness present, and I saw no reason for objection.

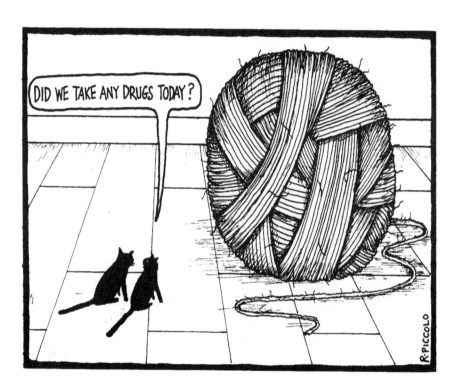

Dianne Reum

Denny Derbyshire

Leslie Ewing

Mary Lawton

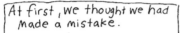

for Heather and Pete

At first, we thought we had made a mistake.

"We didn't want an armadillo— we wanted a cat!"

But then we realized it was just a weight distribution problem.

For awhile, excersise in the apartment helped.

– get down!

But that only increased the already ravenous appetite

So when the refrigerator lock was mysteriously picked,

We knew it was time for a diet.

Here you go! Cling peaches and cottage cheese!

Lawton

Rina Piccolo

Nicole Hollander

Ursula Roma

"I have to close now— Mr. Muffins feels we need to process."

Lee Kennedy

Do cats always see things you can't see
when you're on your own, it's late, and
there's something scary on TV?

"TIME FOR MY FAVORITE SOAP OPERA:
'NINE LIVES TO LIVE.' "

She found him in the parking lot of the **Trekkie** Convention... She decided he was Part Siamese... and Part Vulcan...

Denny Derbyshire

"It's taken me years... but I now have one in every color!"

Cinders McLeod

Mette Thomsen

Chris Suddick

Diane DiMassa

About The Editor

Roz Warren is the editor of fifteen collections of women's humor, including *Men are from Detroit, Women are from Paris*, and *Women's Lip*. She reviews humor books and CDs for numerous publications, and is working on her first novel. She lives with her son, Thomas, in Bala Cynwyd, Pennsylvania.

Women's Lip

Outrageous,
Irreverent
and Just
Plain
Hilarious
Quotes

Edited by ROZ WARREN

Alternating between the outrageous, the irreverent and the just plain hilarious, *Women's Lip* quotes over 500 of the wildest, sassiest things women have ever said. This brash collection is a fantastic gift for a girlfriend, sister or mother—or just for you when you could use a snappy quote or a good laugh.

On Ego:
"Listen, everyone is entitled to my opinion."
   —Madonna

On Womanhood:
"We haven't come a long way, we've come a short way.
If we hadn't come a short way, no one would be calling us 'baby.'"

—Elizabeth Janeway

ISBN 1-887166-38-6; $7.95 U.S.

Hysteria books are available at book and gift stores everywhere, or by calling 630-961-3900.

Men are from Detroit, Women are from Paris is a collection of cartoons that has women poking fun at all those qualities they love to hate but can't live without. Nicole Hollander (syndicated cartoonist of "Sylvia") ia among the contributing artists.

ISBN 1-887166-51-3; $7.95 U.S.

My Cat's Not Fat, He's Just Big Boned is an all-new cartoon collection from "Sylvia" cartoonist Nicole Hollander. Featuring cats who hypnotize their owners, cats who plot dastardly deeds but get distracted, and of course cats obsessed with food, food, food. This hilarious compilation is just right for kitty-lovers everywhere.

ISBN 1-887166-43-2; $9.95 U.S.

Hysteria books are available at book and gift stores everywhere, or by calling 630-961-3900.

"I don't think so!"

The Inner Bitch calls it as she sees it. Author Elizabeth Hilts heralds an end to Toxic Niceness and arms women with the highly effective phrase, "I don't think so," which she applies with grace, wit and humor to myriad situations.

ISBN 1-9629162-0-X; $8.95 U.S.

Hysteria books are available at book and gift stores everywhere, or by calling 630-961-3900.

The Bitch Is Back!

The Inner Bitch is back, this time taking on love and romance. New from the bestselling author of *Getting in Touch with Your Inner Bitch*, this guide to the Inner Bitch Way of Intimacy is a whole new way to look at love!

ISBN 1-887166-44-0; $8.95 U.S.

Hysteria books are available at book and gift stores everywhere, or by calling 630-961-3900.